Words of Love

WORDS
of LOVE

EDITED BY
TINA REED

A PERIGEE BOOK

The author wishes to thank
Bertha, David, Bob, and Nancy.

•

Perigee Books
are published by
The Putnam Publishing Group
200 Madison Avenue, New York, NY 10016

Library of Congress
Cataloging-in-Publication Data

Words of love / edited by Tina Reed. — 1st Perigee ed.
p.   cm.
1. Love—Quotations, maxims, etc.   I. Reed, Tina.
PN6084.L6W66   1993   92-31593 CIP

ISBN 0-399-51789-8

Cover photo © by H. Armstrong Roberts, Inc.
Printed in the United States of America
1 2 3 4 5 6 7 8 9 10

This book is printed on acid-free paper.
∞

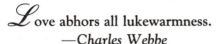

*L*ove abhors all lukewarmness.
—*Charles Webbe*

·

JAQUES: Rosalind is your love's name?
ORLANDO: Yes, just. . . .
JAQUES: What stature is she of?
ORLANDO: Just as high as my heart.
—*William Shakespeare*

·

The best smell is bread, the best savour
salt, the best love that of children.
—*Proverb*

·

If I had to live my life over again, I'd
choose the same parents, the same
birthplace . . . the same wife.
—*H. L. Mencken*

·

I love you as New Englanders love pie!
—*Don Marquis*

$\mathscr{C}$onstancy in love is perpetual inconstancy, inasmuch as the heart is drawn to one quality after another in the beloved, now preferring this, now that. Constancy is therefore inconstancy held in check and confined to the same object.
—*La Rochefoucauld*

·

I thank all who have loved me in
their hearts,
With thanks and love from mine.
—*Elizabeth Barrett Browning*

·

We love the things we love
for what they are.
—*Robert Frost*

·

Love makes hard hearts gentle.
—*Proverb*

*N*o, the heart that has truly lov'd
    never forgets,
  But as truly loves on to the close,
As the sun-flower turns on her god,
    when he sets,
  The same look which she turn'd
    when he rose.
          —*Thomas Moore*

.

Keep your eyes wide open before
marriage, and half shut afterwards.
          —*Proverb*

.

When she had passed, it seemed like the
  ceasing of exquisite music.
  —*Henry Wadsworth Longfellow*

.

Love is a good teacher, he teaches
    in no time.
      —*Pierre Corneille*

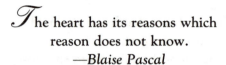

*T*he heart has its reasons which
reason does not know.
—*Blaise Pascal*

·

There is a lady sweet and kind,
Was never face so pleased my mind;
I did but see her passing by,
And yet I love her till I die.
—*Anonymous (fr. Thomas Ford)*

·

Love is always open arms. If you close
your arms about love, you will find that
you are left holding only yourself.
—*Leo Buscaglia*

·

A married couple are well suited when
both partners usually feel the need for a
quarrel at the same time.
—*Jean Rostand*

*P*arting is all we know of heaven,
And all we need of hell.
—*Emily Dickinson*

•

Sex is one of the nine reasons
for re-incarnation . . . The other eight
are unimportant.
—*Henry Miller*

•

Come live with me, and be my love,
And we will some new pleasures prove
Of golden sands and crystal brooks
With silken lines, and silver hooks.
—*John Donne*

•

I love the idea of there being
two sexes, don't you?
—*James Thurber*

$\mathcal{T}$here is no commitment in the world
like having children.
—*Bill Cosby*

.

Together they can long endure,
Yet once they are separated
The hazel dies almost at once,
The honeysuckle very soon.
"My darling, it is so with us:
No you without me, no me without
you!"
—*Marie de France*

.

At last I know what love is really like.
—*Virgil*

.

For I'm not so old, and not so plain,
And I'm quite prepared to marry again.
—*Sir W. S. Gilbert*

$\mathscr{C}$hildren are a poor man's riches.
—*Proverb*

.

Love, *n*. A temporary insanity curable
by marriage or by removal of the patient
from the influences under which he
incurred the disorder. This disease, like
caries and many other ailments, is
prevalent only among civilized races
living under artificial conditions;
barbarous nations breathing pure air and
eating simple food enjoy immunity from
its ravages.
—*Ambrose Bierce*

.

The omnipresent process of sex, as it is
woven into the whole texture of our
man's or woman's body, is the pattern
of all the process of our life.
—*Havelock Ellis*

$\mathcal{B}$reathless, we flung us on the windy
hill,
Laughed in the sun, and kissed the
lovely grass.
　　　—*Rupert Brooke*

·

There is no certainty in love, especially
these days. Therefore pressing to find
out if someone "really cares" is always a
mistake. If you have to ask, you don't
want to hear the answer.
　　—*Judith Martin (Miss Manners)*

·

In marriage do thou be wise; prefer the
person before money; virtue before
beauty; the mind before the body.
　　　—*William Penn*

·

Whoso loves believes the impossible.
　　—*Elizabeth Barrett Browning*

*L*ove that's wise
Will not say all it means.
—*Edwin Arlington Robinson*

.

To be in love is merely to be in a state
of perceptual anesthesia—to mistake an
ordinary young man for a Greek god or
an ordinary young woman for a goddess.
—*H. L. Mencken*

.

Over the mountains and over the
    waves,
Under the fountains and under the
    graves;
Under floods that are deepest, which
    Neptune obey,
Over rocks that are steepest, Love will
    find out the way.
—*Anonymous*

A smile that glowed
Celestial rosy red, love's proper hue.
—*John Milton*

.

On that last New Year's Eve and all the
eves that went before it, there was
Eternity and Beauty, infinite, boundless
loveliness and content.
—*George Bernard Shaw*

.

A lover whose passion is extreme
Loves even the faults of his beloved.
—*Molière*

.

Love is the answer, but while you're
waiting for the answer, sex raises some
pretty good questions.
—*Woody Allen*

*N*ear and far, near and far,
  I am happy where you are;

  Likewise I have never learnt
  How to be it where you aren't.
  —*Ogden Nash*

.

Love doesn't grow on the trees like
apples in Eden—it's something you have
to make. And you must use your
imagination to make it too, just like
anything else. It's all work, work.
  —*Joyce Cary*

.

Tomorrow may he love who never
loved before, and may he who has loved
love too.
  —*Anonymous (Latin)*

.

Love is, above all, the gift of oneself.
  —*Jean Anouilh*

$\mathscr{B}$e with me darling, early and late.
    Smash glasses—
I will study wry music for your sake.
For should your hands drop white and
    empty
All the toys of the world would break.
        —John Frederick Nim

·

True love is like ghostly apparitions:
everybody talks about them but few
    have ever seen one.
      —La Rochefoucauld

·

Love conquers all; let us too
    surrender to Love.
      —Virgil

·

Love is a flame;—we have beaconed
    the world's night.
      —Rupert Brooke

$\mathcal{O}$ love is the crooked thing,
  There is nobody wise enough
  To find out all that is in it,
  For he would be thinking of love
  Till the stars had run away
  And the shadows eaten the moon.
      —*William Butler Yeats*

.

Entreat me not to leave thee, or to
return from following after thee: for
whither thou goest, I will go; and where
thou lodgest, I will lodge: thy people shall
be my people, and thy God my God.
      —*The Bible*

.

Then since we mortal lovers are,
  Ask not how long our love will last;
But while it does, let us take care
  Each minute be with pleasure past. *passed.*
      —*Sir George Etherege*

*A*s your wedding ring wears, your cares
will wear away.
—*Proverb*

·

Love is like quicksilver in the hand.
Leave the fingers open and it stays.
Clutch it, and it darts away.
—*Dorothy Parker*

·

To be in love with someone who
doesn't love back gives you a pain in the
chest at night.
—*Benny Hill*

·

With you there is life and joy and peace
and all good things—away from you there
is turmoil and anguish and blank despair.
—*Bertrand Russell*

$\mathscr{O}$f peace and quiet we sometimes
 grow weary,
But never of loving or being loved.
 —*Vicomte de Parny*

·

True love never grows old.
 —*Proverb*

·

Only tell her that I love:
 Leave the rest to her and Fate:
Some kind planet from above
May perhaps her pity move:
 Lovers on their stars must wait.—
Only tell her that I love!
 —*John Cutts*

·

The real secret [of a successful marriage]
is not in finding the right mate but in
 being the right mate.
 —*Jane E. Brody*

*M*arriage is popular because it combines the maximum of temptation with the maximum of opportunity.
—*George Bernard Shaw*

·

Love is a game in which both players cheat.
—*Proverb*

·

Age cannot wither her, nor custom stale
Her infinite variety. Other women cloy
The appetites they feed, but she makes hungry
Where most she satisfies.
—*William Shakespeare* *Antony &*
Cleopatra?

·

I kissed my first girl and smoked my first cigarette on the same day. I haven't had time for tobacco since.
—*Arturo Toscanini*

A house without woman and firelight,
is like a body without soul or sprite.
—*Benjamin Franklin*

·

There can be no true goodness nor true
love without the utmost clear-sightedness.
—*Albert Camus*

·

We find delight in the beauty and
happiness of children that makes the
heart too big for the body.
—*Ralph Waldo Emerson*

·

When you are in love with someone you
want to be near him all the time, except
when you are out buying things and
charging them to him.
—*Miss Piggy*
(according to Henry Beard)

$\mathscr{C}$onstancy in love is of two kinds: one comes from continually finding new things to love in the beloved, and the other from making it a point of honour to remain constant.
—*La Rochefoucauld*

·

A successful marriage is an edifice that must be rebuilt every day.
—*André Maurois*

·

When in love we often doubt what we most believe.
—*La Rochefoucauld*

·

Develop confidence and the ability to feel love, hope and faith, and acquire a strong will to live.
—*Norman Cousins*

*W*estern Wind, when wilt thou blow,
The small rain down can rain?
Oh, if my love were in my arms
And I in my bed again.
—*Ballad*

.

If music be the breakfast food of love,
kindly do not disturb until lunch time.
—*James Agee*

.

One cannot live what he does not
dedicate himself to. To dedicate yourself
to love you must be forever growing
in love.
—*Leo Buscaglia*

.

You can keep your first lover a long time
provided you do not take a second.
—*La Rochefoucauld*

*N*ear you nothing of my old self
remains,
And your love has made me a virgin.
—*Victor Hugo*

.

Variability is one of the virtues of a
woman. It obviates the crude
requirements of polygamy. If you have
one good wife you are sure to have a
spiritual harem.
—*G. K. Chesterton*

.

There's nothing half so sweet in life
As love's young dream.
—*Thomas Moore*

.

A sudden impulse that cannot be defined
At times takes hold of us and makes
us love.
—*Pierre Corneille*

$\mathscr{T}$here will always be a battle between
the sexes because men and women want
different things. Men want women and
women want men.
—*George Burns*

.

Such is the power of love in gentle mind,
That it can alter all the course of kind.
—*Edmund Spenser*

.

Marriage resembles a pair of shears, so
joined that they can not be separated;
often moving in opposite directions, yet
always punishing anyone who comes
between them.
—*Sydney Smith*

.

I shall love you in December
With the love I gave in May!
—*John Alexander Joyce*

I chose my wife, as she did her wedding-gown, not for a fine glossy surface, but such qualities as would wear well.
—*Oliver Goldsmith*

.

Keep love in your heart. A life without it is like a sunless garden when the flowers are dead. The consciousness of loving and being loved brings a warmth and richness to life that nothing else can bring.
—*Oscar Wilde*

.

The plural of spouse is spice.
—*Christopher Morley*

.

Love delights in praise.
—*Proverb*

*A*ll mankind love a lover.
—*Ralph Waldo Emerson*

·

Then wrong not, dearest to my heart,
My true, though secret, passion:
He smarteth most that hides his smart,
And sues for no compassion.
—*Sir Walter Raleigh*

·

A lady's imagination is very rapid; it
jumps from admiration to love, from
love to matrimony in a moment.
—*Jane Austen*

·

Lovers are madmen.
—*Proverb*

·

Hell, Madame, is to love no longer.
—*Georges Bernanos*

$\mathscr{M}$y heart is like a singing bird
    Whose nest is in a watered shoot;
My heart is like an apple-tree
    Whose boughs are bent with thick-set
       fruit;
My heart is like a rainbow shell
    That paddles in a halcyon sea;
My heart is gladder than all these,
    Because my love is come to me.
            —*Christina Rossetti*

·

A man without a wife is but half a man.
            —*Proverb*

·

Call no man foe, but never
    love a stranger.
    —*Stella Benson*

·

No human creature can give orders to love.
          —*George Sand*

"*Love* seeketh not Itself to please,
"Nor for itself hath any care,
"But for another gives its ease,
"And builds a Heaven in Hell's despair."
—*William Blake*

·

Love is an endless mystery for it has
nothing to explain it.
—*Rabindranath Tagore*

·

Having a child is surely the most
beautifully irrational act that two people
in love can commit.
—*Bill Cosby*

·

Absence is to love as wind is to fire;
It extinguishes the small and kindles
the great.
—*Roger de Bussy-Rabutin*

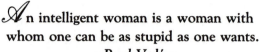

$\mathscr{A}$n intelligent woman is a woman with whom one can be as stupid as one wants.
—*Paul Valéry*

.

How many loved your moments
    of glad grace,
And loved your beauty with love
    false or true;
But one man loved the pilgrim soul
    in you,
And loved the sorrows of your
    changing face.
        —*William Butler Yeats*

.

The most human thing we have to do in life is to learn to speak our honest convictions and feelings and live with the consequences. This is the first requirement of love.
—*Father William Du Bay*

$\mathcal{M}$ an attributes holiness to his faith in
the same way as he believes in the
beauty of the one he loves.
—*Ernest Renan*

·

It is a certain sign of love to want
to know, *to relive,* the childhood
of the other.
—*Cesare Pavese*

·

Love and you shall be loved. All love is
mathematically just, as much as the two
sides of an algebraic equation.
—*Ralph Waldo Emerson*

·

Beauty's but an offensive dart:
It is not armour for the heart.
—*Sir George Etherege*

$\mathscr{A}$ good wife and health are a man's
best wealth.
—*Proverb*

·

Lovers' quarrels renew their love.
—*Terence*

·

As unto the bow the cord is,
So unto the man is woman,
Though she bends him, she obeys him,
Though she draws him, yet she follows,
Useless each without the other.
—*Henry Wadsworth Longfellow*

·

It's [charm] a sort of bloom on a
woman. If you have it, you don't need
to have anything else; and if you don't
have it, it doesn't much matter what
else you have.
—*J. M. Barrie*

M an often thinks he is in control when he is being controlled, and while his mind is striving in one direction his heart is imperceptibly drawing him in another.
—*La Rochefoucauld*

·

What we think is less than what we know: What we know is less than what we love: What we love is so much less than what there is; and to this precise extent, we are much less than what we are.
—*R. D. Laing*

·

Love, free love, cannot be bound
To any tree that grows on ground.
—*William Blake*

·

With all thy faults, I love thee still.
—*William Cowper*

*U*ncertainty and ambiguity are as
exciting in courtship as they are tedious
in marriage.
—*Judith Martin (Miss Manners)*

.

Not everyone who understands his own
mind understands his heart.
—*La Rochefoucauld*

.

There is no prince or prelate
I envy—no, not one.
No evil can befall me—
By God, I have a son!
—*Christopher Morley*

.

The first obligation of a genuinely loving
person will always be to his or her
marital and parental relationships.
—*M. Scott Peck, M.D.*

*L*OVE has nothing to do with what
you are expecting to get—only with
what you are expecting to give—
which is everything.
—*Katharine Hepburn*

.

Earth's the right place for love;
I don't know where it's likely to go
better.
—*Robert Frost*

.

Ah Love! could thou and I with
    Fate conspire
To grasp this sorry Scheme of Things
    entire,
    Would not we shatter it to bits—
    and then
Re-mould it nearer to the Heart's
    Desire!
—*Omar Khayyám*

"*L*ove," she said, "seems to pump me full of vitamins. It makes me feel as if the sun were shining and my hat was right and my shoes were right and my frock was right and my stockings were right, and somebody had just left me ten thousand a year."
—*P. G. Wodehouse*

·

A good husband makes a good wife.
—*Proverb*

·

Love is like war: easy to begin but very hard to stop.
—*H. L. Mencken*

·

Love, all alike, no season knows, nor clime,
Nor hours, days, months, which are the rags of time.
—*John Donne*

*T*he pleasure of love is loving, and we
get more happiness from the passion we
feel than from the passion we inspire.
—*La Rochefoucauld*

.

She never should have looked at me
If she meant I should not love her!
—*Robert Browning*

.

Women have served all these centuries
as looking-glasses possessing the magic
and delicious power of reflecting the
figure of man at twice its natural size.
—*Virginia Woolf*

.

The meeting of two personalities is like
the contact of two chemical substances:
if there is any reaction, both are
transformed.
—*Carl Jung*

$\mathcal{T}$o love, and to be loved, is the greatest
happiness of existence.
—*Sidney Smith*

.

. . . Marriage is so much more
interesting than divorce,
Because it's the only known example of
the happy
meeting of the immovable object
and the
irresistible force.
—*Ogden Nash*

.

Scientists are discovering at this very
moment that to live as if to live and love
were one is the only way of life for
human beings.
—*Ashley Montagu*

$\mathcal{L}$et your love see me even through
the barrier of nearness.
—*Rabindranath Tagore*

·

She gave me eyes, she gave me ears;
And humble cares, and delicate fears;
A heart, the fountain of sweet tears;
And love, and thought, and joy.
—*William Wordsworth*

·

Any time that is not spent
on love is wasted.
—*Torquato Tasso*

·

Is not old wine wholesomest, old
pippins toothsomest, old wood burn
brightest, old linen wash whitest? Old
soldiers, sweethearts, are surest, and
old lovers are soundest.
—*John Webster*

*B*ecause genuine love involves an extension of oneself, vast amounts of energy are required.
—M. Scott Peck, M.D.

.

I thought to find Love in the heat of day,
But sweet Love is the Comforter of Night.
—*William Blake*

.

Every man who is high up likes to feel that he has done it all himself; and the wife smiles, and lets it go at that. It's our only joke. Every woman knows that.
—*J. M. Barrie*

.

The sound of a kiss is not so loud as that of a cannon, but its echo lasts a great deal longer.
—*Oliver Wendell Holmes*

*S*ee how she leans her cheek upon her
    hand!
  O, that I were a glove upon that hand,
  That I might touch that cheek!
        —*William Shakespeare*

.

How many times do I love again?
  Tell me how many many beads
    there are
    In a silver chain
    Of evening rain,
Unravelled from the tumbling main,
  And threading the eye of a yellow star:—
So many times do I love again.
        —*Thomas Lovell Beddoes*

.

My sister! my sweet sister! if a name
Dearer and purer were, it should be thine.
        —*Lord Byron*

$\mathcal{T}$he joy of life is variety; the tenderest love requires to be renewed by intervals of absence.
—*Samuel Johnson*

.

Infatuation is when you think that he's as sexy as Robert Redford, as smart as Henry Kissinger, as noble as Ralph Nader, as funny as Woody Allen and as athletic as Jimmy Connors. Love is when you realize that he's as sexy as Woody Allen, as smart as Jimmy Connors, as funny as Ralph Nader, as athletic as Henry Kissinger and nothing like Robert Redford—but you'll take him anyway.
—*Judith Viorst*

.

Love must be learned, and learned again and again; there is no end to it.
—*Katherine Anne Porter*

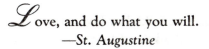

$\mathscr{L}$ove, and do what you will.
—*St. Augustine*

·

Where love is, no disguise can hide
it for long; where it is not, none can
simulate it.
—*La Rochefoucauld*

·

I arise from dreams of thee
In the first sweet sleep of night,
When the winds are breathing low,
And the stars are shining bright.
—*Percy Bysshe Shelley*

·

You must always be a-waggle
with LOVE.
—*D. H. Lawrence*

·

Be warm but pure; be amorous but chaste.
—*Lord Byron*

I can't be talkin' of love, dear,
I can't be talkin' of love.
If there be one thing I can't talk of
That one thing do be love.

But that's not sayin' that I'm not lovin'—
Still water, you know, runs deep,
An' I do be lovin' so deep, dear,
I be lovin' you in my sleep.
                    —*Esther Mathews*

.

Oh, promise me that some day you and I
Will take our love together to some sky
Where we can be alone and faith renew,
And find the hollows where those
              flowers grew.
                    —*Clement Scott*

.

That Love is all there is,
Is all we know of Love.
                    —*Emily Dickinson*

*W*e are one, after all, you and I, together
we suffer, together exist, And forever
will recreate each other.
—*Teilhard de Chardin*

.

I love thee with the breath,
Smiles, tears, of all my life!—and if God
choose,
I shall but love thee better after death.
—*Elizabeth Barrett Browning*

.

Had it any been but she,
And that very face,
There had been at least ere this
A dozen dozen in her place.
—*Sir John Suckling*

.

Love is and was my lord and king.
—*Alfred, Lord Tennyson*

*I*n a happy marriage it is the wife
who provides the climate, the husband
the landscape.
—*Gerald Brenan*

.

There is only one kind of love, but there
are a thousand copies, all different.
—*La Rochefoucauld*

.

Beauty has graced you since your early
years,
Nor will it leave you at the close of life;
Time justly proud of having formed
your face
Will not allow its loveliness to fade.
—*François Maynard*

.

Hearts are not had as a gift but
hearts are earned.
—*William Butler Yeats*

*I*t's curious how, when you're in love, you yearn to go about doing acts of kindness to everybody.
—*P. G. Wodehouse*

•

For, in my mind, of all mankind
I love but you alone.
—*Ballad*

•

Are not religion, love and music three expressions of the same thing, the need to expand one's self is the lifework of all noble souls.
—*Honoré de Balzac*

•

Escape me?
Never—
Beloved!
While I am I, and you are you.
—*Robert Browning*

$\mathcal{L}$ove is not all; it is not meat nor drink
Nor slumber nor a roof against the rain.
—*Edna St. Vincent Millay*

·

Absence sharpens love, presence
strengthens it.
—*Thomas Fuller*

·

If we are to love we must extend
ourselves to adjust our communication
to the capacities of our beloved.
—*M. Scott Peck, M.D.*

·

I'd be crazy to propose to her, but when
I see that profile of hers I feel the only
thing worth doing in the world is to grab
her and start shouting for clergymen and
bridesmaids to come running.
—*P. G. Wodehouse*

$\mathcal{S}$he walks in beauty, like the night
Of cloudless climes and starry skies;
And all that's best of dark and bright
Meet in her aspect and her eyes.
　　　　　—*Lord Byron*

·

Kissing your hand may make you feel
very, very good, but a diamond and
sapphire bracelet lasts forever.
　　　　　—*Anita Loos*

·

Where there is no trust, there is no love.
　　　　　—*Proverb*

·

Trusty, dusky, vivid, true,
With eyes of gold and bramble dew,
Steel-true and blade-straight
The great artificer
Made my mate.
　　　　　—*Robert Louis Stevenson*

All thoughts, all passions, all delights,
Whatever stirs this mortal frame,
All are but ministers of Love,
And feed his sacred flame.
—Samuel T. Coleridge

·

When you really want love you will find
it waiting for you.
—Oscar Wilde

·

Husbands are married for better or
worse—but not for lunch.
—Erma Bombeck

·

Oh, when I was in love with you,
Then I was clean and brave,
And miles around the wonder grew
How well did I behave.
—A. E. Housman

$\mathcal{O}$ne must not be mean with the
affections; what is spent of the fund is
renewed in the spending itself.
—*Sigmund Freud*

·

I was a child and *she* was a child,
In this kingdom by the sea,
But we loved with a love that was more
than love—
I and my Annabel Lee.
—*Edgar Allan Poe*

·

'Tis better to have loved and lost, than
never to have loved at all.
—*Samuel Butler*

·

Ah, my Beloved, fill the Cup that clears
TODAY of past Regrets and future Fears.
—*Omar Khayyám*

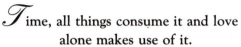

$\mathscr{T}$ime, all things consume it and love
alone makes use of it.
—*Paul Claudel*

.

In hours of bliss we oft have met:
They could not always last;
And though the present I regret,
I'm grateful for the past.
—*William Congreve*

.

Clarity of mind means clarity of passion,
too; this is why a great and clear mind
loves ardently and sees distinctly what
he loves.
—*Blaise Pascal*

.

Four be the things I'd been better
without:
Love, curiosity, freckles, and doubt.
—*Dorothy Parker*

*T*he reason why lovers never tire of each other's company is that the conversation is always about themselves.
—*La Rochefoucauld*

·

When marrying, ask yourself this question: Do you believe that you will be able to converse well with this person into your old age? Everything else in marriage is transitory.
—*Friedrich Nietzsche*

·

O! how this spring of love resembleth
The uncertain glory of an April day.
—*William Shakespeare*

·

Love is an irresistible desire to be irresistibly desired.
—*Robert Frost*

$\mathcal{G}$ive all to love;
  Obey thy heart;
  Friends, kindred, days,
  Estate, good fame,
  Plans, credit, and the Muse—
  Nothing refuse.
    —*Ralph Waldo Emerson*

You love me so much, you want to put
            me in your pocket.
            —*D. H. Lawrence*

                    .

The typical example of Gift-love would
be that love which moves a man to work
        and plan and save for the future
well-being of his family which he will die
without sharing or seeing; of the second
[Need-love], that which sends a lonely
or frightened child to its mother's arms.
            —*C. S. Lewis*

$\mathscr{T}$hat's the thing about girls. Every time they do something pretty, even if they're not much to look at, or even if they're sort of stupid, you fall half in love with them, and then you never know *where* the hell you are.
—J. D. Salinger

.

I have spread my dreams under your feet;
Tread softly because you tread on my dreams.
—*William Butler Yeats*

.

Marrying a man is like buying something you've been admiring for a long time in a shop window. You may love it when you get it home, but it doesn't always go with everything else in the house.
—*Jean Kerr*

$\mathcal{L}$et me not to the marriage of true
   minds
Admit impediments. Love is not love
Which alters when it alteration finds,
Or bends with the remover to remove.
   —*William Shakespeare*

.

Love has always been the most
important business in my life, or rather
the only one.
   —*Stendhal*

.

He who does good comes to the temple
gate, he who loves reaches the shrine.
   —*Rabindranath Tagore*

.

In the human heart, love is
the torrid zone.
   —*Jacques-Henri Bernardin de
   Saint-Pierre*

$\mathcal{T}$hrough all the years of my marriage,
my love for Camille, like my stomach,
has steadily grown.
—*Bill Cosby*

.

So sweet love seemed that April morn,
When first we kissed beside the thorn,
So strangely sweet, it was not strange
We thought that love could never change.
—*Robert Bridges*

.

The power our loved ones have over us
is almost always greater than the power
we have over ourselves.
—*La Rochefoucauld*

.

I do not love him because he is good,
but because he is my little child.
—*Rabindranath Tagore*

Dad
10/30/03
for 80th
BD
celeb.

*H*ereafter in a better world than this,
I shall desire more love and knowledge
of you.
—*William Shakespeare*

.

Love makes up for the lack of long
memories by a sort of magic. All other
affections need a past: love creates a past
which envelops us, as if by enchantment.
—*Benjamin Constant*

.

Sing we for love and idleness,
Naught else is worth the having.
—*Ezra Pound*

.

I did but look and love awhile,
'Twas but for one half-hour;
Then to resist I had no will,
And now I have no power.
—*Thomas Otway*

$\mathscr{F}$ind the seed at the bottom of your
heart and bring forth a flower.
   —*Shigenori Kameoka*

·

The noble fire which blazes in my heart
   for you
Will find all possible, and the impossible
   easy.
   —*Jean de Rotrou*

·

It is a truth universally acknowledged,
that a single man in possession of a good
fortune, must be in want of a wife.
   —*Jane Austen*

·

It is as absurd to say that a man can't
love one woman all the time as it is to
say that a violinist needs several violins
to play the same piece of music.
   —*Honoré de Balzac*

*L*ove rules the court, the camp,
    the grove,
And men below, and saints above;
For love is heaven, and heaven is love.
        —Sir Walter Scott

.

If ever two were one, then surely we.
If ever man were loved by wife, then
    thee;
If ever wife was happy in a man,
Compare with me ye women if you can.
        —Anne Bradstreet

.

Hunger and love are the two axes on
which the world turns. Humanity is
ruled completely by love and hunger.
        —Anatole France

*T*rue Love doesn't know the meaning of
renunciation, is not even aware of that
problem, never resigns itself.
—*Eugene Ionesco*

·

We love being in love, that's
the truth on't.
—*William M. Thackeray*

·

DEAR ABBY: Can you please tell me
where the custom of kissing a lady's
hand originated? And why?
—*Charles*

DEAR CHARLES: It originated in France,
and since a person has to start
somewhere, that's as good a place as any.
—*Abigail Van Buren*

·

Forever wilt thou love, and she be fair!
—*John Keats*

$\mathcal{H}$ ere are fruits, flowers, leaves
and branches
And here is my heart which beats only
for you.

—*Anatole France*

.

Love not me for comely grace,
For my pleasing eye or face,
Nor for any outward part;
No, nor for a constant heart!
For these may fail or turn to ill:
So thou and I shall sever.
Keep therefore a true ~~woman's~~ eye,
And love me still, but know not why!
So hast thou the same reason still
To doat upon me ever.

—*Anonymous*

.

Love may be delightful, but even more
so are the ways in which it reveals itself.

—*La Rochefoucauld*

$\mathcal{T}$o live is like to love—all reason is
against it, and all healthy instinct for it.
—*Samuel Butler*

·

Strong are the couples who resort
More to courtship and less to court.
—*Ogden Nash*

·

Love decentralizes, truth universalizes: he
who speaks addresses all mankind, he who
loves incarnates all mankind in himself.
—*Eugen Rosenstock-Huessy*

·

For love, all love of other sights
controls,
And makes one little room, an
everywhere.
—*John Donne*

$\mathcal{T}$ hose graceful acts, those
thousand decencies,
That daily flow from all her words
and actions.
—*John Milton*

·

Pride leaves the heart the day
that love enters it.
—*Théophile Gautier*

·

There is no such thing as an old woman.
Any woman, at any age, if she loves
and if she is good, will give a man a
moment of infinity.
—*Jules Michelet*

·

Grief can take care of itself, but to get
the full value from joy you must have
somebody to divide it with.
—*Mark Twain*

O, my luve is like a red, red rose
That's newly sprung in June.
O, my luve is like the melodie
That's sweetly play'd in tune.
—*Robert Burns*

•

We forgive so long as we love.
—*La Rochefoucauld*

•

Pride, virtue, riches, all must yield.
When love speaks, he is the master.
—*Pierre Carlet de Chamblain*
de Marivaux

•

There is no love where there is no will.
—*Mahatma Gandhi*

•

Love is blind.
—*Proverb*

$\mathcal{H}$e'll live his days where the sunbeams
     start
 Nor could storm or wind uproot him.
My own dear love, he is all my heart—
And I wish somebody'd shoot him.
      —*Dorothy Parker*

·

If intelligence were taken out of my life,
it would only be more or less reduced. If
I had no one to love, it would be ruined.
      —*Henry De Montherlant*

·

Is love an art? Then it requires
knowledge and effort.
      —*Erich Fromm*

·

A mother is not a person to lean on, but
a person to make leaning unnecessary.
      —*Dorothy Canfield Fisher*

$\mathcal{O}$h, let the clouds grow dark above,
　　My heart is light below;
'Tis always summer when we love,
　　However winds may blow;
And I'm as proud as any prince,
　　All honors I disdain:
She says I am her *rain beau* since
　　I kissed her in the rain.
　　　　　—*Samuel Minturn Peck*

·

'Tisn't beauty, so to speak, nor good
　talk necessarily. It's just IT. Some
women'll stay in a man's memory if they
　　once walked down a street.
　　　　—*Rudyard Kipling*

·

Never seek to tell thy love
Love that never told can be;
For the gentle wind does move
Silently, invisibly.
　　　　—*William Blake*

This being in love is great—you get a lot of compliments and begin to think you are a great guy.
—F. Scott Fitzgerald

.

Come, let us now resolve at last
To live and love in quiet;
We'll tie the knot so very fast
That Time shall ne'er untie it.
—John Sheffield, Duke
of Buckinghamshire

.

Our wanting to love, our yearning for love, our loving itself becomes an addiction.
—Robin Norwood

.

See how love and murder will out.
—William Congreve

$\mathscr{L}$ove does not dominate; it cultivates.
—*Johann Wolfgang von Goethe*

.

In youth, it was a way I had
　to do my best to please
And change with every passing lad
　to suit his theories.
　　—*Dorothy Parker*

.

Love is a talkative passion.
—*Bishop Thomas Wilson*

.

To see her is to love her,
And love but her forever;
For nature made her what she is,
And ne'er made sic anither!
　　—*Robert Burns*

$\mathscr{M}$y true love hath my heart, and I have
    his,
By just exchange one for another given.
I hold his dear, and mine he cannot miss,
There never was a better bargain driven.
    —*Sir Philip Sidney*

.

What is love? . . . It is the morning
    and the evening star.
    —*Sinclair Lewis*

.

An archeologist is the best husband a
woman can have; the older she gets, the
    more interested he is in her.
    —*Agatha Christie*

.

Love does not consist in gazing at
each other but in looking together in
    the same direction.
    —*Antoine de Saint-Exupéry*

*W*here love rules, there is no will to
power; and where power predominates,
there is love lacking. The one is the
shadow of the other.
—*Carl Jung*

.

Ever the wide world over, lass,
Ever the trail held true,
Over the world and under the world,
And back at the last to you.
—*Rudyard Kipling*

.

Marriage has many pains, but celibacy
has no pleasures.
—*Samuel Johnson*

.

Only God, my dear,
Could love you for yourself alone
And not your yellow hair.
—*William Butler Yeats*

$\mathcal{L}$ove is too young to know what
  conscience is;
Yet who knows not conscience is born
  of love?
  —*William Shakespeare*

.

The particular charm of marriage is the
duologue, the permanent conversation
between two people who talk over
everything and everyone till death breaks
the record. It is this back-chat which, in
the long run, makes a reciprocal equality
more intoxicating than any form of
servitude or domination.
  —*Cyril Connolly*

.

Build with lithe love. With love
  like lion-eyes.
With love like morningrise,
With love like black, our black.
  —*Gwendolyn Brooks*

*I*t is difficult to define love; what can be said is that in the soul it is a passion to dominate another, in the mind it is a mutual understanding, whilst in the body it is simply a delicately veiled desire to possess the beloved after many rites and mysteries.
—*La Rochefoucauld*

.

No spring, nor summer beauty hath such grace,
As I have seen in one autumnal face.
—*John Donne*

.

My love is fair, my love is gay,
As fresh as bin the flowers in May.
—*George Peele*

.

A good wife makes a good husband.
—*Proverb*

*S*atisfaction in individual love cannot be
attained without the capacity to love
one's neighbor, without true humility,
courage, faith and discipline.
—*Erich Fromm*

.

Be plain in dress, and sober in your diet;
In short, my deary, kiss me, and be quiet.
—*Lady Mary Wortley Montagu*

.

So long as we love we serve; so long as
we are loved by others, I would almost
say that we are indispensable.
—*Robert Louis Stevenson*

.

A maiden marries to please her parents;
a widow to please herself.
—*Proverb*

*C*ome live with me and be my love,
And we will all the pleasures prove
That hills and valleys, dales and field,
Woods, or steepy mountains yield.
—*Christopher Marlowe*

·

I have never changed underneath my
changing moods; I have never stopped
loving God, my father, and freedom.
—*Madame de Staël*

·

If you'd be loved, be worthy
to be loved.
—*Ovid*

·

To me, fair friend, you never can be old
For as you were when first your eye I
eyed,
Such seems your beauty still.
—*William Shakespeare*

$\mathcal{G}$ive me a kiss, and to that kiss a score;
Then to that twenty, add a hundred more:
A thousand to that hundred: so kiss on,
To make that thousand up a million.
Treble that million, and when that is
     done,
Let's kiss afresh, as when we first begun.
         —*Robert Herrick*

·

The perfect lover is one who turns
    into a pizza at 4:00 A.M.
       —*Charles Pierce*

·

Half light, half shade,
She stood, a sight to make an old man
    young.
       —*Alfred, Lord Tennyson*

·

When love is greatest, words are fewest.
        —*Proverb*

I have pursued fame always in the
hope of winning love.
—*Madame de Staël*

.

Feed the flame on the altar of the ideal,
Guide the people to the good by way of
the beautiful,
By way of admiration and love for
woman.
—*Théophile Gautier*

.

Of all forms of caution, caution in love
is perhaps the most fatal to true
happiness.
—*Bertrand Russell*

.

I wonder by my troth, what thou, and I
Did, till we loved?
—*John Donne*

M arriage, to women as to men,
must be a luxury, not a necessity; an
incident of life, not all of it.
—*Susan B. Anthony*

·

None shall part us from each other,
One in life and death are we:
All in all to one another—
I to thee and thou to me!
—*Sir W. S. Gilbert*

·

In war as in love, one must meet
eye-to-eye to reach an end.
—*Napoleon Bonaparte*

·

There is only one science, love, only one
riches, love, only one policy, love. To
make love is all the law, and the prophets.
—*Anatole France*

*D*EAR ABBY: What factor do you think
is the most essential if a woman is to
have a lasting marriage?
                          —*Dotty*

DEAR DOTTY: A lasting husband.
                 —*Abigail Van Buren*

·

There is a garden in her face
Where roses and white lilies grow;
A heavenly paradise is that place
Wherein all pleasant fruits do flow.
                    —*Thomas Campion*

·

Faults are thick where love is thin.
                          —*Proverb*

·

I could not love thee, Dear, so much,
Loved I not honour more.
                    —*Richard Lovelace*

That best portion of a good man's life,
His little, nameless, unremembered acts
Of kindness and of love.
—*William Wordsworth*

·

Marriage, *n*. The state or condition of a
community consisting of a master, a
mistress and two slaves, making in all,
two.
—*Ambrose Bierce*

·

If thou must love me, let it be for nought
Except for love's sake only.
—*Elizabeth Barrett Browning*

·

If we go anywhere we'll go together to
meet what happens,
May-be we'll be better off and blither,
and learn something.
—*Walt Whitman*

*I*n love I pay my endless debt to
  thee for what thou art.
  —*Rabindranath Tagore*

.

To be a woman is to have the same
  needs and longings as a man.
We need love and we wish to give it.
  —*Liv Ullmann*

.

My love in her attire doth show
  her wit,
  It doth so well become her:
For every season she hath dressings fit,
  For winter, spring, and summer.
  No beauty she doth miss,
  When all her robes are on:
  But Beauty's self she is,
  When all her robes are gone.
  —*Ballad*

*T*he angels . . . singing unto one
    another,
Can find among their burning terms of
    love,
None so devotional as that of "mother."
    —*Edgar Allan Poe*

.

A woman without a man cannot meet a
    man, any man, of any age, without
    thinking, even if it's for a half-second,
    Perhaps this is *the* man.
    —*Doris Lessing*

.

But we always return
To our first loves.
—*Charles-Guillaume Étienne*

.

Grow old along with me! The best
is yet to be.
—*Robert Browning*

I will make you brooches and toys
  for your delight
Of birdsong at morning and starshine
  at night.
  —*Robert Louis Stevenson*

·

Love is space and time made directly
  perceptible to the heart.
  —*Marcel Proust*

·

The proof of gold is fire; the proof
of woman, gold; the proof of man,
  a woman.
  —*Benjamin Franklin*

·

For five whole years I've seen her every
  day,
And each time think I see her for the
  first time.
  —*Jean Racine*

$\mathcal{H}$ere with a Loaf of Bread beneath
     the Bough,
A Flask of Wine, a Book of Verse—
     and Thou
  Beside me singing in the Wilderness—
And Wilderness is Paradise enow.
          —Omar Khayyám

·

We do not live in accordance with our
   mode of thinking, but we think in
   accordance with our mode of loving.
          —V. V. Rozinov

·

Love unreturned is like a question
        without an answer.
          —Proverb

·

Love is enough: though the
     World be a-waning.
          —William Morris

*H*usbands are indeed an irritating form
      of life,
And yet through some quirk of
      Providence most of
      them are really very deeply ensconced
      in the
      affection of their wife.
                    —*Ogden Nash*

.

The pleasures and the cares of ambitious
      goals attained, even with boundless
      power, are nothing beside the intimate
      happiness to be found in affection
                    and in love.
                    —*Stendhal*

.

All love is sweet,
Given or returned.
Common as light is love,
And its familiar voice wearies not ever.
                    —*Percy Bysshe Shelley*

$\mathscr{B}$elieve me, if all those endearing young
    charms
Which I gaze on so fondly today,
Were to change by tomorrow and fleet
    in my arms,
Like fairy gifts fading away,
Thou would'st still be adored as this
    moment thou art,
Let thy loveliness fade as it will,
And around the dear ruin each wish
    of my heart
Would entwine itself verdantly still.
        —Thomas Moore

·

It is good to love the unknown.
        —Charles Lamb

·

Love is what you've been through
    with somebody.
        —James Thurber

*Y*et love, mere love, is beautiful indeed
And worthy of acceptation.
— *Elizabeth Barrett Browning*

·

Sexuality throws no light upon love, but
only through love can we learn to
understand sexuality.
— *Eugen Rosenstock-Huessy*

·

The wine of Love is music,
  And the feast of Love is song:
And when Love sits down to the
  banquet,
Love sits long.
— *James Thomson*

·

Say "I love you" to those you love.
The eternal silence is long enough to
be silent in.
— *George Eliot*

$\mathscr{L}$ove is staying awake all night with a sick child, or a very healthy adult.
—*David Frost*

.

She is a winsome wee thing,
She is a handsome wee thing,
She is a lo'esome wee thing,
   This sweet wee wife o' mine.
—*Robert Burns*

.

To live with someone and to live in someone are two fundamentally different matters. There are people in whom one can live without living with them, and vice versa. To combine both requires the purest degree of love and friendship.
—*Johann Wolfgang von Goethe*

.

Familiar acts are beautiful through love.
—*Percy Bysshe Shelley*

$\mathcal{W}$hat is a kiss? Why this, as some
approve:
The sure, sweet cement, glue, and lime
of love.
—*Robert Herrick*

·

Love many things, for therein lies the
true strength, and whosoever loves much
performs much, and can accomplish
much, and what is done in love is well
done.
—*Vincent van Gogh*

·

Two things prolong life—a quiet heart
and a loving wife.
—*Proverb*

·

When Silence speaks for Love
she has much to say.
—*Richard Garnett*

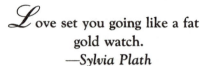

$\mathscr{L}$ove set you going like a fat
gold watch.
—*Sylvia Plath*

.

She was as good as she was fair,
None—none on earth above her!
As pure in thought as angels are:
To know her was to love her.
—*Samuel Rogers*

.

Love, like fire, cannot survive without
continual movement, and it ceases to live
as soon as it ceases to hope or fear.
—*La Rochefoucauld*

.

Amoebas at the start
Were not complex;
They tore themselves apart
And started Sex.
—*Arthur Guiterman*

$\mathcal{I}$n the spring a young man's fancy
lightly turns to thoughts of love.
—*Alfred, Lord Tennyson*

.

Husbands are like fires. They go out
if unattended.
—*Zsa Zsa Gabor*

.

My dear and only love, I pray
This noble word of thee,
Be governed by no other sway
But purest monarchy.
—*James Graham, Marquis of Montrose*

.

Marriage is an act of will that signifies
and involves a mutual gift, which unites
the spouses and binds them to their
eventual souls, with whom they make up
a sole family—a domestic church.
—*Pope John Paul II*

*T*wo persons must believe in each other, and feel that it *can* be done and *must* be done; in that way they are enormously strong.

—*Vincent van Gogh*

.

Who kissed her toes?
Who d'you s'pose?
And also her nose?
I kissed her toes. . . .

Who clasped her tight?
That wasn't right.
Oh, the delight!
I clasped her tight.

—*George Bernard Shaw*

.

O, love's best habit is in
seeming trust.

—*William Shakespeare*

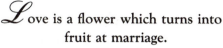

*L*ove is a flower which turns into
fruit at marriage.
—*Proverb*

·

Give a man a girl he can love,
  As I, O my love, love thee;
And his heart is great with the pulse of
  Fate,
  At home, on land, on sea.
—*James Thomson*

·

What is it men in women do require?
The lineaments of Gratified Desire.
What is it women do in men require?
The lineaments of Gratified Desire.
—*William Blake*

·

Love sought is good, but giv'n
unsought is better.
—*William Shakespeare*

*T*here isn't any formula or method. You
learn to love by loving—by paying
attention and doing what one thereby
discovers has to be done.
—*Aldous Huxley*

.

Drink to me only with thine eyes,
And I will pledge with mine;
Or leave a kiss but in the cup
And I'll not look for wine.
—*Ben Jonson*

.

Sex and beauty are inseparable, like life
and consciousness. And the intelligence
which goes with sex and beauty, and
arises out of sex and beauty, is intuition.
—*D. H. Lawrence*

.

The head is always fooled by the heart.
—*La Rochefoucauld*

O lyric Love, half angel and half bird,
And all a wonder and a wild desire.
—*Robert Browning*

.

Grace was in all her steps, heaven in her
    eye,
In every gesture dignity and love.
—*John Milton*

.

The taste of the first kiss disappointed
me like a fruit tasted for the first time. It
is not in novelty, it is in habit that we
find the greatest pleasures.
—*Raymond Radiguet*

.

We can't form our children on our own
concepts; we must take them and love
them as God gives them to us.
—*Johann Wolfgang von Goethe*

$\mathscr{O}$f all the things that I would rather,
It is to be my daughter's father.
—*Ogden Nash*

•

Neither a lofty degree of intelligence
nor imagination nor both together go to
the making of genius. Love, love, love,
that is the soul of genius.
—*Wolfgang Amadeus Mozart (attr.)*

•

Misses! the tale that I relate
This lesson seems to carry—
Choose not alone a proper mate,
But proper time to marry.
—*William Cowper*

•

Kiss, *n.* A word invented by the poets as
a rhyme for "bliss."
—*Ambrose Bierce*